PENNSYLVANIA INSPIRED LEADERSHIP

A Roadmap for American Educators

Ben Wood Johnson

PENNSYLVANIA INSPIRED LEADERSHIP

A ROADMAP FOR AMERICAN EDUCATORS

BEN WOOD JOHNSON

TESKO PUBLISHING

Middletown, Pennsylvania

BEN WOOD POST

www.benwoodpost.com

Pennsylvania Inspired Leadership

A Roadmap for American Educators

BEN WOOD JOHNSON

Tesko Publishing/My Eduka Solutions

Middletown, Pennsylvania
Tesko Publishing

Johnson, Ben Wood

Pennsylvania Inspired Leadership: A Roadmap for American Educators/Ben Wood Johnson. — Tesko Publishing ed.

Includes bibliographical references and index.

ISBN-13: 978-1-948600-13-2 (pbk.)

ISBN-10: 1-948600-13-7

This book, or aspects thereof, was first published in 2010

The information illustrated in this book was compiled for a school project. The analysis is based on class notes and other materials.

Johnson, Ben Wood
Pennsylvania Inspired Leadership: A Roadmap for American Educators
Tesko Publishing website address: www.benwoodjbooks.com

Eduka Solutions
330 W. Main St. #214
Middletown, PA 17057, USA

Printed in the United States of America

Cover Illustration by Wood Oliver

For Jean Robert,
        whose passion for education inspired my
        incessant thirst for learning

TABLE OF CONTENTS

FOREWORD

This book is about professional development in education. The analysis presented herein centers on the use of standards in public schools. The text examines the popular program commonly known as the *Pennsylvania Inspired Leadership Standards*, also known as *PIL* or *PILS* for short.

The text explores, although not in-depth, the use of professional development standards in the Keystone State. While the manuscript is not exhaustive, it is concise. It is informative. The book could serve as a guide for educators in various aspects of education, including, but not limited to, administration, leadership, and management.

The manuscript contains seven chapters. They are brief. They focus on a number of salient issues in educational administration and leadership.

Chapter 1 examines how the PIL standards came about. Chapter 2 explores how the PIL applies to school leadership. Chapter 3 discusses how the PIL addresses professional development issues. Chapter 4 explores the structure of the program. Chapter 5 examines program requirements. Chapter 6 explores the role of local entities in implementing the PIL standards. Chapter 7 examines, though superficially, the degree to which funding issues could hamper the PIL initiatives.

Good Reading!
Ben Wood Johnson, Ph.D.
Pennsylvania, USA
July 2019

ACKNOWLEDGMENTS

THIS BOOK IS a reformatted version of a school paper, which I completed in 2010. I would like to thank my son *Woodner* for his comments and suggestions on all aspects of this work. I would also like to thank *Xaon* for his inputs during the editing phase. I would like to echo a special *thank you* to those who contributed to this work. Thank you all.

Keywords: Pennsylvania Inspired Leadership, K-12 education, elementary education, school leadership, school development, and standards

Education is the key for success. However, success is not always an outcome of education.

— *BWJ 2013*

INTRODUCTION

Several years ago, the Commonwealth of Pennsylvania adopted a professional development curriculum known as the inspired leadership initiatives. The program was extremely popular during the time of its adoption. It soon became a template for school leadership development across the region.

As the name indicates, the program was geared towards reforming school leadership. It established administrative standards for school professionals across the Commonwealth. It was dubbed the PIL or PILS. I will use both acronyms interchangeably in the present document.

This text provides an historical context for the creation of the PIL. It assesses expectations. It examines existing leadership standards.

Pennsylvania is proactive in the domain of school leadership. The PIL program is a great example to illustrate that assertion. Other states are also making a substantial headway in the domain.

In recent years, a number of states adopted approaches, which are similar to the PIL initiatives. Some of these approaches have been designed to address professional improvements in school, particularly at the local level. Others were designed to address administrative problems in education in general. Various states have passed legislatures and/or policies, which address how educators should go about designing and/or implementing professional development initiatives in their schools.

The book has its limits. For instance, it does not explore the PIL standards at length. That being said, it is a comprehensive assessment of the foundation of the program. It examines how Pennsylvania legislators structured the mechanism for the adoption of educational leadership initiatives across the Commonwealth.

The book provides a snapshot about administrative initiatives in the domain of school leadership. But it is not exhaustive. The same, the text is not based on an empirical survey. If you want to learn about recent initiatives taken by the Commonwealth of Pennsylvania in the domain of school leadership, please visit the Pennsylvania Department of Education's official website.[1]

This book could become a guide for anyone in the field of education. It is a roadmap for school administrators, educators, and other professionals. The content it features is valuable not only for educators across Pennsylvania, but also for professionals in other regions. It could become a valuable addendum to your personal library. Without further a due, let us get to it.

---

[1] You can find important information about the PIL program by visiting the following link:
http://www.education.pa.gov/Teachers - Administrators/PA Inspired Leaders/Pages/default.aspx

CHAPTER ONE

CREATION OF THE PIL
STANDARDS

In the late 1990s, the Commonwealth of Pennsylvania developed a professional reform agenda known as the "Inspired Leadership Initiatives." The program is officially known as the Pennsylvania Inspired Leadership Standards. It is also known as PILS, for short.

In most educational settings, the program is identified as PIL. Throughout this document, I will refer to the program as PIL as well. Let us delve in the practical side of the program.

The PIL initiatives are essentially a statewide (standards-based) continuing professional education for schools and system leaders ("PA Inspired Leadership," n.d.). The pervading understanding is that professional development for new principals and assistant principals has often been neglected when it comes to other teaching professions (Burk, 2012). The PIL was designed to bridge that gap.

One-way of looking at the program is that a leader must be equipped with the correct skills and the *savoir-faire,* which he or she could earn only through the PIL standards. The leader would be able to develop the knowledge, the skills, and the *"know-how"* necessary so he or she could become effective in both administrative and pedagogical tasks. How did the PIL standards come about? Let us review the history of this initiative.

BRIEF HISTORY OF ACT 45

The Pennsylvania Inspired Leadership initiatives emanated from a legislative act, which is known as

Act 45. The act provided the legal framework for the PIL standards. In addition, the act set up the framework for other initiatives.

Act 45 was originally adopted in 2007. As will discuss later, Act 45 is the amended version of Act 48, which had been adopted in 1999. The contents of Act 48 emanated from a 1949 Act. This act was known as the Public School Code of 1949 (P.L. 30, No. 14) ("Bill Information - House Bill 842; Regular Session 2007-2008," n.d.).

Act 45 was designed as a filtering mechanism (or a triage) for potential educational employees in Pennsylvania. The act allowed background checks for both already employed individual and perspective employees. It was construed as a means or as a way to weed out people with questionable characters, including people who had been convicted of certain offenses.

Act 45 was designed to identify school employees who got into trouble with the law. It was designed to rid the schools of people who misbehaved, while employed as an educator. The act further made it possible for school administrators to identify employees who had been convicted of certain offenses ("Bill Information - House Bill 842; Regular Session 2007-2008," n.d.).

Act 45 was designed to help school officials get rid of employees who had been convicted of inappropriate conducts, while in charge of school affairs, such as school finances. Similarly, the act made it possible to train assistant superintendents for eligibility. The act targeted education professionals across the Commonwealth.

The act set the requirements to become an educator. It set qualifications for new employees. It established the criteria for transferred programs and classes.

The act targeted teachers seeking certification for program of continuing professional education. The act provided continuing professional education for school or systems leaders. It established school leadership standards across Pennsylvania. In this case, it is the foundation of the creation of the PIL program itself. Act 45 settled standards for pupils, school attendance, school lunch, and breakfast repayment, among other administrative issues.

ACT 45 AND THE DEPARTMENT OF EDUCATION

The act established the duties of the Department of Education about school health services and other educational aid programs. The act set the limits for early learning programs, including Head Start Supplemental Assistance Program; it also settled the Pennsylvania Pre-K Counts Program.

Act 45 established the limits for aiding distressed school districts and student attendance in other districts. It set standards for opportunities to achieve educational excellence across the Commonwealth. The act determined the responsibilities of the department and State Board of Education.

The act created professional standards for education empowerment. It gave superintendents the power to recommend dismissal. The act settled standards for education empowerment districts and boards of control for specific school districts.

The act set community education councils and provided guidelines for State funding. It established the Pennsylvania Technical College Program. It set the limits for educational improvements (tax credit

11

terms). The act further provided the basis for funding public libraries.

The 1999 Act established repayment from the Commonwealth to local school districts. It established the limits for small district aid. The act established the basic education funding for the school year. The act provided payments for limited English competency programs. It provided payments to intermediate units and earmarked payments for special education to school districts.

Act 45 created a means for budget stabilization plan (progress report). It provided payments for pupil transport. The act set the limits for the Commonwealth to pay back charter schools and cyber charter schools. The act further established the Pennsylvania accountability grants.

CHAPTER TWO

THE PILS AND SCHOOL
LEADERSHIP

The PIL standards were designed to empower Pennsylvania school leaders. The standards would allow the leader the capacity to incorporate problem-solving experiences to the position (Burk, 2012). He or she would be able to use data as a tool or an instrument to take actions that would simplify school improvement (Burk, 2012).

The skills acquired from the program would in turn help the leader improve the design of means for an up-to-date delivery of instructions. The newly acquired skills would help the leader develop the means necessary to foster an environment conducive to teaching and learning for both teachers and students (Wilson, n.d.). The previous understanding is extirpated from the Act 45 law itself, which requires all principals, assistant principals, superintendents, and assistant superintendents to earn 180 clock hours (According to the requirements of the Act 48 PIL) continuing professional hours within a five-year hiring cycle ("Pennsylvania Inspired Leadership (PIL) - The School District of Philadelphia," n.d.).

The idea behind passing the PIL was to build capacity among school leaders. The expectation is that school administrators would be forced to focus solely on events that could lead to efficient practices. In this case, I am referring to practices that, in a sequel, could yield real results in the schools. But such practices must also lead to student achievement, preferably in failing schools (Wilson, n.d.).

Another expectation is that effective school leaders would have a great impact on student achievement (Wilson, n.d.). This view is seemingly based on the notion that research-based education is the way of the future. The understanding here is that every school leader throughout the Commonwealth of Pennsylvania must uphold such practices (Wilson, n.d.).

PURPOSE OF THE PIL STANDARDS

The PIL program was seemingly designed as a means or as a strategy to underline on the *Dos* and *Don'ts* of direct instructional improvements. The program was possibly crafted to promote long-term improvements within the schools. It was irrefutably designed to enhance student achievement.

The PIL initiatives are supposed to help leaders develop the capacity to improve student achievement (Pennsylvania Department of Education, n.d.). The program was designed with the expectation that it would help change the status quo in various public schools. Another expectation worth noting is that the program would help leaders in schools that consistently fail in both federal and state administered tests to focus on the development of the capacity of leaders to improve student achievement in those schools (Pennsylvania Department of Education, n.d.).

It could further be said that the PIL program was designed to afford leaders in those failing schools the tools necessary to address the problems within their school. To this day, the results are mixed about the scope (or even the effects) of the program. Regardless, few people have questioned the effectiveness of the PIL standards in certain regions, surpassingly when it comes to suburban areas.

At this point, let me say that there is not a clear consensus in the debate, which addresses the importance of the PIL standards. The same, I do not examine the potential worth of the program here. Nonetheless, it might be hasty to ignore important points of the debate. Let us explore two important issues here.

First, it is not clear whether the program has had any positive effect on failing schools. The amplitude to which the program helped instill strong leadership initiatives in most struggling school districts is uncertain. The Commonwealth is not doing well in school performance. For instance, when it comes to failing schools, Pennsylvania is among the worst states in the nation.[2]

Second, it is unclear about the degree to which the program's implementation made a big difference in school leadership. The argument often echoed is that most school districts do not always hire individuals within their respective localities or regions for administrative positions, such as superintendent, principals, or assistant principals. Some of the leaders that evolve within a number of Pennsylvania schools are not exigently natives of the Commonwealth itself or the region.

LEADERSHIP AS AN ACQUIRED SKILL

An epistemological argument is worth pointing out in this text. Leadership is not an acquired skill. Some people are natural leaders. They know instinctively how to behave in certain situations. Therefore, the PIL program might not play a substantial role in their success or the lack thereof.

---

[2] See my other works section to learn more about this topic.

Other assessments about the program are worthy of mention here. It is well understood that the PIL has been helpful in most school districts. The view across-the-board is that this program has had a significant impact in helping school districts improve the quality of their leadership team. The understanding is that the PIL has had a positive impact on various school districts across the Commonwealth.

An important understanding worth pointing out as well is that in many school districts, the PIL program has led to an increase of excellence in leadership quality. For most observers, implementing the program has been a success. The program attracted stacks of professionals into the field of education, many observers have argued. Overall, the PIL program is believed to have increased the knowledge base of most school administrators across the Keystone State.

CHAPTER THREE

THE PILS AND PROFESSIONAL DEVELOPMENT

The PIL program affords both newly hired and experienced school administrators the professional development and the support they might need so that they could increase student achievement statewide ("Professional Learning / PA Inspired Leadership (PIL)," n.d.). In recent years, a number of studies examined the scope of the PIL initiatives. For instance, a popular study found that new building principals require professional development experience to navigate the task and responsibilities that are often associated with being a building principal (Burk, 2012). The PIL initiatives had been designed to provide the necessary tools to school leaders so that they could perform their duties with ease.

Another study found out that most schools require proactive leaders. The widely held belief is that professional development for school principals and assistant principals could inculcate the need to challenge the status quo within the school. As an important initiative, the PIL program could help school leaders stir their schools in the right direction. The understanding is that the PIL is valuable tool in educational leadership. As such, it would allow school leaders to strive for real change.

Another study examined the scope to which the PIL program showed the way leaders, notably school principals and assistant principal behaved in urban schools. The study found the PIL had an impact on the practices espoused by school principals to a point where these practices inevitably influenced teachers, which, in turn, influenced student performance (Dinkins, 2009). For most observers, the PIL initiatives are very valuable to school professionals, students, and parents alike.

But to reiterate, there is no consensus as to the role of the federal government on the PIL initiatives.

THE NCLB AND THE PIL STANDARDS

The PIL standards predate the NCLB ("Bill Information - House Bill 842; Regular Session 2007-2008," n.d.).[3] I discuss the effects of this piece of legislation in more detail later in the text. I explore the role of the federal government in state educational matters in more detail in my other works on the subject. Still, it would be unwise to overlook any link between these two initiatives.

Within the context of the NCLB, which mandated all students should achieve a competence level on state testing by the year 2014, Pennsylvania school officials are professedly well positioned to receive valuable skills and the knowledge, which are necessary for their school to comply with federal expectations ("Professional Learning / PA Inspired Leadership (PIL)," n.d.). It must be noted that this

---

[3] This understanding is based on the language contains in several pieces of legislatures.

view is mostly prevalent among supporters of the PIL program.

As of 2016, the long-term effects of the PIL standards are still unsettled. Nonetheless, most educators in Pennsylvania believe the program has had some positive impacts on administrative staff members. They have been able to recruit qualified professionals to turn around their school.

By and large, the PIL is regarded as a success in various regions throughout the Commonwealth. It must also be noted that there are objections about the substantive nature of the PIL standards. For example, not everyone believes that this program had a significant impact on school leadership.

The argument is that other causes could contribute either to good practices or to bad habits. Some observers have contended that crediting school success to professional development measures such as the PIL is simply shortsighted. I must admit that I avoided exploring the PIL standards from this angle in the present work.

TARGETED PROFESSIONALS

Act 48 was passed in 1999 ("ACT 48," n.d.). But it went in full effect in the year 2000. As of July 1 of the aforementioned year, officials in education required all educational professionals within the Commonwealth to comply with Act 45/Act 48 PIL credit.

As already discussed in this text, Act 45 is the amended version of Act 48 ("Act 45 - PA Inspired Leaders (PIL) - PaTTAN," n.d.).[4] It was adopted in the year 2007 (Wilson, n.d.). This piece of legislation was introduced under the House Bill 842, during regular session (2007-2008) ("Bill Information - House Bill 842; Regular Session 2007-2008," n.d.).

Pennsylvania educators, patently those who hold Pennsylvania approved public school certifications, must take part in professional education initiatives as a condition to keep their certification. The same rules apply to new administrators as well.

---

[4] The Act 48 was amended in 2007. The amended version is known as Act 45.

As a rule, the PIL only targets practitioners in the education profession throughout the Commonwealth. As of January 1, 2008, all active schools and system leaders were expected to comply with the expectations of Act 45/Act 48 PIL. These acts demands administrative, supervisory, letters of eligibility, and vocational certificates holders to take part in continuing professional education ("ACT 48," n.d., p. 48).

To comply with Act 48, school professionals must complete one of the followings:

1. The professional must complete 6 credits (college-level courses)
    a. Each collegiate study credit equal to 30 hours in the classroom
2. The professional must complete 180 hours of continuing professional education programs
    a. This may include educational related events or learning experience
3. The professional must complete a combination of college credits, continuing education courses, or other approved programs, events or learning experience, which equal to 180 clock hours

The expectations from the PIL chiefly concern individuals who are employed in several types of positions. These positions include, but are not limited to, the ones listed in Table 3.[5] Nonetheless, the PIL standards are considered the most available means for school leaders in Pennsylvania to set up consistent professional improvements throughout the region.

Within the last few years, the PIL standards have been implemented across the Commonwealth. But as noted earlier, the results are mixed about their effects on school leadership. The impacts of these initiatives are unsettled. Put differently, the immediate role of the PIL standards in helping school leaders improve their schools remain unclear. To that extent, the debate is still brewing regarding the real effects of the PIL standards.

Despite the implementation of the PIL, a number of issues are worth pointing out in the debate. Across the Commonwealth of Pennsylvania, for instance, many school districts are considered in dire need of improvement. But the extent to which

---

[5] Note: The above information had been retrieved from the Lehigh University, College of Education website.

the PIL is the solution is unsettled. This is to say that the jury is still out about the impact of the PIL standards, particularly when it comes to initiatives, which are designed to turn failing school around.

I must echo that I do not evaluate the scope of the PIL program in the present work. Nonetheless, the information relayed here has been modeled as a means to inspire the reader to explore the PIL further. Let me also reiterate that this book does not delve in the details of the gist of the PIL program.

Table 3: List of Employee Positions

- ✓ **Superintendent**
- ✓ **Assistant Superintendent**
- ✓ **Area Vocational-Technical School Director**
- ✓ **Intermediate Unit Executive Director**
- ✓ **Intermediate Unit Assistant Executive Director**
- ✓ **Principal**
- ✓ **Assistant and Vice Principal**
- ✓ **Instructional I**
- ✓ **Instructional II**
- ✓ **Educational Specialist I**
- ✓ **Educational Specialist II**

The program affects educators who hold administrative certificates. The understanding is that these people must be employed in any of the positions listed above, at least as of January 1, 2008. On 2016, the PIL standards were still in effect across the Commonwealth of Pennsylvania.

It must be reiterated that the effects of those standards are unsettled. Understandings are mitigated as to the real impact of the PIL standards. But there is enough evidence to suggest that the program has not yielded tangible results in portions of the Commonwealth, including, but not limited to, urban and rural areas. In many of these places, there is a dearth of qualified leadership in charge of the schools, notably in struggling school districts.

Certainly, the debate is raging as to the true nature of the reason (or the causes) these schools are struggling. But the commonly held view is that schools that struggle academically also tend to struggle financially. Chapter 7 examines the financial issue, though not at length.

It could be said that most Pennsylvania schools are struggling. Some schools (or some school districts) are failing for panoply of reasons. But for most observers, school leaders are to blame for their inability to turn failing schools (or their school districts) around. It could also be said that other causes, which are not always under a particular school leader's control, could explain the cause of the drawbacks, which a number of Pennsylvania schools seem to be experiencing.

CHAPTER FOUR

DECIPHERING THE PIL PROGRAM

The PIL is a comprehensive, cohort-based program, which focuses on developing the leadership capacity of school leaders ("Act 45 - PA Inspired Leaders (PIL) - PaTTAN," n.d.). The objective of this initiative is to improve school performance, which would in turn lead to school improvement and student achievement ("PA Inspired Leadership (PIL) Program," n.d.).

The PIL program requires participants to enroll in leadership-oriented courses. But the mandatory course names and the number of credit hours must almost include Pennsylvania Department of

Education approved courses. 6 The next few paragraphs will outline a list of several possible courses and their suggested credit hours ("Shippensburg University – Registrar – Act 48 ACT 45 PIL Credit," n.d.).

Please keep in mind that there is more to the PIL standards than the information outlined in the present text. Also, bear in mind that the information showed here is not based on any official sources. I did not recover such information from official platforms or from official educational entities. The views explained in these pages are not based on updated data from official sources.[7]

---

[6] Note: The above information had been retrieved from the Shippensburg University website.

[7] The information listed below had been retrieved from a corollary of educational-related sources, including websites and other reputable higher education institutions. Please note the information addressing the number of credit hours needed to comply with the PIL standards had been retrieved from the Shippensburg University's official website.

PIL COMPULSORY COURSES

- ➢ Practicum in Central Office Administration
  - ✓ 3-6 Credit Hours
- ➢ The Legal Side of Public School Administration
  - ✓ 3 Credit Hours
- ➢ Educational Leadership, Policy, and Governance
  - ✓ 3 Credit Hours
- ➢ Educational Facilities and Plant Management
  - ✓ 3 Credit Hours
- ➢ Business and Finance in Public Education
  - ✓ 3 Credit Hours
- ➢ School and Community Relations
  - ✓ 3 Credit Hours
- ➢ Negotiation and Personnel Management in Public Education
  - ✓ 3 Credit Hours
- ➢ Curriculum Theory and Development
  - ✓ 3 Credit Hours
- ➢ Leadership for Pupil Services
  - ✓ 3 Credit Hours

Core And Corollary Standards

The understanding here is that superintendents and school principals must be prepared based on the aforementioned standards. The program apply to both current and future candidates who hold or wish to hold a certificate as principals, vice principals, or assistant principals anywhere throughout the Commonwealth of Pennsylvania. As will discuss in the next section, the Pennsylvania department of education covers the cost of the program for individuals or for any school entity within the Commonwealth.

The PIL program was designed to change aspects of Pennsylvania school leadership and professional development. It is supposed to address nine core issues about leadership. They are divided as follows: three "core" leadership standards and six "corollary" standards ("Standards - Pennsylvania Inspired Leadership Initiative," n.d.).

The fundamental mission of this program is to instill a climate for growth and support of school leaders. To carry out that goal, the program is consisted of several standards. The next paragraphs highlight the essentiality of these standards.

THREE CORE STANDARDS

The core standards are as follows:
1. The leader has the knowledge and skills to think and plan strategically; he must create an organizational vision around personalized student success.
2. The leader is grounded in standards-based systems theory and knowledge to his or her job as the architect of standards-based reform in the school.
3. The leader knows how to access and use suitable data to tell decision-making at all levels of the system.

SIX COROLLARY STANDARDS

The PIL program includes several corollary standards. They are as follows:
1. The leader creates a culture of teaching and learning with an emphasis on learning.

2. The leader manages resources for effective results.
3. The leader collaborates, communicates, engages, and empowers others inside and outside the organization to continue excellence in learning.
4. The leader manages in a fair and equitable manner with personal and professional dignity.
5. The leader advocates for children and public education in the larger political, social, economic, legal, and cultural context.
6. The leader supports professional growth of self- and others through practice and inquiry.

In sum, the underlining premise of the previously outlined standards is that they would inspire leaders to be fully committed to the educational process. Another argument worth pointing out is that the PIL program is important for the success of struggling schools. Most schools in Pennsylvania are expected to adopt the PIL standards as a condition for a number of benefits, particularly at the state level.

CHAPTER FIVE

PROGRAM ADMINISTRATION

The PIL program is managed by the Pennsylvania Department of Education, in partnership with the Pennsylvania Intermediate Units and other entities throughout the Commonwealth ("PA Inspired Leadership (PIL) Program," n.d.). The program is offered at eight regional sites (*See* Figure 5.1).

Each site supports an array of cohort groups (Wilson, n.d.). These sites offer the following: (1) A comprehensive curriculum, which had been developed by the National Institute for School Leadership (NISC), (2) A Pennsylvania-adopted version of the Total Leaders Curriculum, which had been developed by the Pennsylvania School Leadership Council (PLDC) (Wilson, n.d.).

Pennsylvania Inspired Leadership Regions

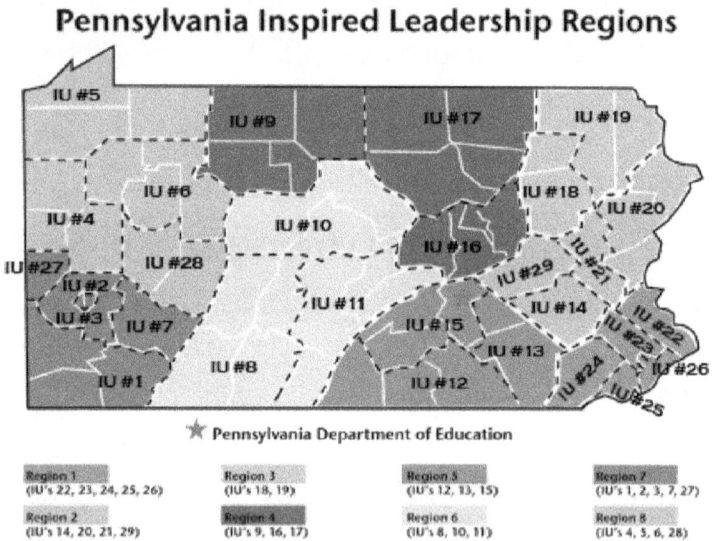

★ Pennsylvania Department of Education

| Region 1 (IU's 22, 23, 24, 25, 26) | Region 3 (IU's 18, 19) | Region 5 (IU's 12, 13, 15) | Region 7 (IU's 1, 2, 3, 7, 27) |
| Region 2 (IU's 14, 20, 21, 29) | Region 4 (IU's 9, 16, 17) | Region 6 (IU's 8, 10, 11) | Region 8 (IU's 4, 5, 6, 28) |

Figure 5.1 Pennsylvania Inspired Leadership Map

Source: www.education.pa.gov[8]

---

[8] Please note that the above information could be found on the website of the Pennsylvania Department of Education. Please see the bibliography to learn more. ("PA Inspired Leadership (PIL) Program," n.d.)

COMMON CORE VERSUS THE PILS

Is there a difference between common core and the PIL standards? The answer is yes. But there are some similarities and other nuances, which are worth pointing out in the debate.

There is a fundamental difference between the two terms. For instance, common core initiatives are based on a broad understanding of school needs. They tend to apply collectively, particularly at the national level.

The PIL program, on the other hand, is mostly surgical in its target population. The PIL initiatives are targeted. They are geared specifically towards state and/or local educational efforts.

It must also be said that when it comes to educational activities, federal and state initiatives often conflict and crash. In other words, their goals are not always compatible. As already noted, states generally enjoy a constitutional privilege in education.

States have a clear responsibility in educational matters. That responsibility is not necessary universal. This is to say, educational priorities tend to vary across state lines. As a result, observers have regularly called for states to reject common core initiatives (Burke, 2012).

As the name implies, common core standards are wide-ranging in scope. This is by design. They generally include English Language Arts (ELA) and Mathematics (Burke, 2012).

The federal government established national assessments, which are often aligned with the mentioned standards. States, on the other hand, are expected or are usually required, to adhere by those standards each year. Sometimes, they do so to the detriment of local necessities in education.

STATE AND FEDERAL ROLE IN EDUCATION

While education in America is left to states, in this case, the Commonwealth of Pennsylvania, the federal government often plays an important role in educational efforts. State and local entities play a greater role in educational matters. Many states have the last word in educational-related initiatives. This is so by law (that is, the U.S. Constitution) and in practice (that is, traditional practices). The federal government usually relies on other means, including the so-called *"Power of the Purse,"* to influence education.

In general, educational issues are left to states. As inferred earlier, an exclusive state control of educational issues might not be in the best interest of children. For example, the landmark court decision in Brown v. Board of Education (1954) could be illustrative of how states or state-related institutions could fix what might be harmful to the educational well-being of most students (Cornell Law, 2010).[9]

In 1954, the United States Supreme Court overturned a long held belief (or local customs), which allowed local school officials to erect a wedge (that is, a physical barrier) between Caucasian and African-American students. This practice emanated from the notion of "Separate but equal doctrine,"

---

[9] In this landmark Supreme Court ruling, school segregation was outlawed. Please the following link to learn more
https://www.law.cornell.edu/supremecourt/text/347/483

which promoted school segregation and other forms of racially motivated practices.

I will not examine these issues at length here. I have debated these issues in other writings. Please see my other works on the subject of school segregation in America to understand the nature of the debate.

CHAPTER SIX

LOCAL INITIATIVES

Presently, not everyone is thrilled with the federal government in state education. Federal interventions could have a harmful impact on students as well. The understanding is that federal officials could pass policies that could have a negative impact on the educational well-being of American children.

Supporter of the viewpoint previously noted have echoed that the NCLB, which was supposed to bring some form of equity within the educational system, has not yielded the results that most observers expected. In essence, the federal government has failed to make education more equitable across the land. Thus, for most observers, a federal role in education has little or no tangible value, before all else, for minority students.

From a different perspective, the common understanding is the unpredictable decision-making of individual states in educational matters might not be useful for the country as a whole. Often, initiatives in one state could be mirrored in other states. This is generally true whether such initiatives are good or bad. To that extent, there is always a need for a balance approach between federal and state involvements in educational-related initiatives.

ALIGNING WITH NATIONAL STANDARDS

The goal of the Pennsylvania Inspired Leadership program is to instrument a national standard. Defining success must be within the scope of the two categories previously mentioned. To that effect, more work needs to be done to come up with a better solution, be it a common core initiative that does not include or exclude certain realities about education.

The notion of common core standards is based on the idea that such standards might promote real choices in education. The understanding is that such an approach might improve accountability in school administration. The view is that if we know what schools are teaching, it might become easier to gauge their performance level. It might also be easier to fix issues related to student achievement.

For most educators, the PIL is an essential tool. It allows them to improve the quality of education within their schools. The program further offers a roadmap for educational professionals across the Commonwealth to follow and to improve their skills.

There is the presumption that such an approach might offer alternatives to struggling public schools. The PIL standards are geared towards encouraging citizen participation in the process. The PIL initiatives were seemingly designed to have a similar effect on local approaches to education in general.

The PIL is also geared towards encouraging parental involvement. This approach is supposed to have a latent effect. Distinct from other attributions, the PIL standards are directed more towards coaching school leaders as to how to involve the community, including parents in education and the delivery of instruction.

THE PIL AS A GAME CHANGER

There is no doubt that the PIL program is a game changer in education, at least within the corridors of the Commonwealth of Pennsylvania. There is a constant need to change the course of school leadership throughout the State. The PIL initiatives offer the tools necessary to stir leadership-related initiatives in the right direction.

The notion of common core standards inscribe within the context of limiting states from taking one-sided initiatives. It could also be said that the common core approach was designed to promote an inclusive educational delivery process. It is a way of considering other causes that might either hinder or promote student learning. Nonetheless, I must point out that, unlike the PIL initiatives, which essentially focus on school administrators, the notion of common core standards targets students.

By its core essence, the PIL program is a game changer. This approach to educational reform grandly targets the characteristics of the delivery process of instruction. It is a more hands-on approach.

For years, many observers have argued that socioeconomic causes do not affect education in a big way. Nowadays, there is a new approach in the debate. There is a new way to examining the role of external causes on student learning. The belief is that common core standards were designed to help balance out exogenous issues that might hamper student learning, which may include socioeconomic causes at home or in the community.

In any event, it could be said that to this point, the implications of common core initiatives are unclear, at least to most observers. The costs and the benefits associated with carrying out these initiatives are also unknown. Nonetheless, there is a national push to adopt such standards in every aspect of education. Not surprisingly, there are some pushbacks against similar initiatives, notably at the local level.

On the other hand, when it comes to the PIL standards, the Commonwealth of Pennsylvania covers all the costs associated with the program. The PIL could be understood as a state approach to standards, at least as a professional development means. Its fundamental goals are to improve student achievement and school performance.

CHAPTER SEVEN

FUNDING ISSUES AND THE PIL

The Commonwealth of Pennsylvania is facing many issues in the domain of school funding. It is worth noting that other education-related issues are legions across the State. A number of skeptics are concerned about the true effects of the PIL standards on school leadership, notably in schools that struggle to recruit qualified professionals.

While some are convinced that the problems that pervade in the Keystone State in terms of education are financially based, others see them as administrative in nature. But it must be said that most observers consider financial inequities as a serious problem across the State. Even the rise of administrative issues, some are convinced, generally stem from the State's current inequitable funding mechanism.

THE DEBATE

The debate is raging about the true nature of the issues, which affect education across Pennsylvania. While I will not address this aspect of the PIL program here, it is worth noting that many have argued that inequitable funding strategies have had a serious impact in the way public schools across the Commonwealth receive funding. This problem tends to affect the way in which school leaders use available funds. It also affects the way they earmark available resources.

There is no doubt about it; school funding is a major issue across Pennsylvania. Many of the schools that are in need of restructuring are in poor districts areas. In such places, school leaders have fewer financial resources to address school-related issues, including teacher salary, school materials, and other issues.

On the other side of the coin, there are those who do not think that funding is a major issue in Pennsylvania. The argument is that there is a need to prepare school leaders to face important challenges. It is important to prepare them to rise to the occasion. But the jury is still out on the degree to which this is possible at all time.

THE REALITY ON THE GROUND

It would be naïve to overlook the school funding issue across Pennsylvania. Indeed, most schools fare better than others do across the State. This is a reality despite of the implementation of the PIL initiatives.

The funding inequity is a real problem. Because of that reality, many school districts cannot compete with other—often, wealthier—schools within the region, if not across the State. In these cases, the PIL has been ineffective, at least when it comes to school improvement or professional development initiatives.

There is enough evidence to support the view that funding issues and school leadership problems go hand and hand. As inferred earlier, a lack of adequate funding could have incommensurable impacts on school personnel, particularly when it comes to staff retention.

Despite the above understanding, the pervading perception is that Pennsylvania school leaders should be more astute in the way they manage their resources. The widely held belief is that these leaders must have the adequate *"know how,"* which would allow them to address pressing issues. They must develop the *"tact"* necessary to fix their schools. They must be able to do so both academically and administratively. Of course, the degree to which the PIL standards could facilitate that task remains unsettled.

CHAPTER SEVEN

CONCLUSION

Instead of a conclusion, let me point out that the PIL initiatives are more complex than the way I explained it in this work. In a different text, I elaborate further on the gist of the program. In the book titled *How to Fix Pennsylvania School*, I took a practical approach to the PIL standards.

In the mentioned text, I explore how a school leader might strive to improve a failing school district. I focus on both the organizational and the curriculum aspects of school reform. I explore, theoretically of course, a means that may help a school leader address curriculum-related issues in a struggling school. I further elaborate on other practices that may be relevant to turn around a school, which is desperately in need of structural changes.

In the aforementioned text, I develop a mock plan to address the failing school. I do so primarily by referencing the PIL standards. I discuss the steps that might be necessary for carrying out the PIL program.

For the sake of implementing that goal, I explore the manners in which a school administrator, a superintendent, or a principal, should go about setting up an improvement plan in a fictitious school district. I elaborate on the means that would have to be put in place to instrument a good school curriculum. While my goal was to present a practical exploration of the PIL standards, I further outline the implementation process in theory. I strongly recommend you to see this book to learn more about the PIL initiatives.

In sum, the common agreement is the NCLB has failed our students. In many circumstances, the belief is that it may be up to the Commonwealth to intervene and offer the best alternatives. It could reasonably be argued the PIL standards had been inscribed within that context. It is a way for the Commonwealth to take control of its educational projects at an early stage.

REFLECTION

The debate is unsettled as to the true effect of the PIL standards. Many observers have legitimate questions, which are seldom examined in depth. Here, let us reflect of a few inquiries.

Please take the time to reflect on the following ten issues. Bear in mind that there is no right or wrong answer. Let us discuss…

1. What role the federal government should play in education locally?
2. Who would benefit the most from the PIL standards?
3. How important are PIL (required) courses?

4. Are there any negatives (or cons) for the department of education to run the PIL program?

5. What is the purpose of the PIL standards outside of directives set forth by state officials?

6. Is there is genuine need for a program like the PIL initiatives?

7. What role educational institutions could play in making the PIL program more effective?

8. Is the PIL program a good way to measure leadership skills?

9. Is there a link between school finance and leadership?

10. Should school leaders be in charge of school finances?

SOURCES CONSULTED

Act 45 - PA Inspired Leaders (PIL) - PaTTAN. (n.d.).
    Retrieved January 27, 2016, from
    http://www.pattan.net/category/Training/page/ac
    t_45__pil.html

ACT 48. (n.d.). Retrieved January 27, 2016, from
    http://coe.lehigh.edu/otc/act-4548

Bill Information - House Bill 842; Regular Session 2007-
    2008. (n.d.). Retrieved June 18, 2016, from the official
    website for the Pennsylvania General Assembly.
    website:
    http://www.legis.state.pa.us/cfdocs/billinfo/billinf
    o.cfm?syear=2007&sind=0&body=H&type=B&BN=0
    842

Burke, L. (2012). States Must Reject National Education Standards While There Is Still Time. Retrieved May 23, 2016, from http://www.heritage.org/research/reports/2012/04/states-must-reject-national-education-standards-while-there-is-still-time

Burk, R. D. (2012, January 1). *New building level leaders' perceptions: Experiences in the Pennsylvania Inspired Leadership's induction and mentoring program.* ProQuest Dissertations Publishing.

Dinkins, S. P. (2009, January 1). *Preparing leaders for the urban school context: A case study analysis for effective leadership.* ProQuest Dissertations Publishing.

Cornell Law. (2010, August 19). Brown v. Board of Education (1954). Retrieved September 26, 2016, from LII / Legal Information Institute website: https://www.law.cornell.edu/supremecourt/text/347/483

PA Inspired Leadership (PIL) Program. (n.d.). Retrieved January 27, 2016, from http://www.education.pa.gov/Teachers - Administrators/PA Inspired Leaders/Pages/default.aspx

Pennsylvania Inspired Leadership (PIL) - The School District of Philadelphia. (n.d.). Retrieved January 27, 2016, from http://webgui.phila.k12.pa.us/offices/l/leadership /pennsylvania-inspired-leaders-pil

Professional Learning / PA Inspired Leadership (PIL). (n.d.). Retrieved January 27, 2016, from http://www.ciu20.org/Page/234

Shippensburg University – Registrar – Act 48 ACT 45 PIL Credit. (n.d.). Retrieved January 27, 2016, from https://www.ship.edu/Registrar/Act_48_ACT_45_ PIL_Credit/

Wilson, C. (n.d.). PA Inspired Leadership (PIL) Legislation: Frequently Asked Questions (FAQs). Retrieved February 5, 2016, from http://www.dli.state.pa.us/portal/server.pt/gatew ay/PTARGS_0_0_252_0_0_47/http;/pubcontent.stat e.pa.us/publishedcontent/publish/cop_hhs/pde/si ngle_web/programs/programs_o_r/pil/legislation_ faq/legislation_faq.html

ABOUT THE AUTHOR

Ben Wood Johnson, Ph.D.
Dr. Ben W. Johnson is a philosopher and social observer. He writes about law, legal theory, education, public policy, politics, race and crime, and ethics.

Ben Johnson graduated from Penn State University and Villanova University. He worked in law enforcement and attended John Jay College of Criminal Justice.

Ben W. Johnson also enjoys reading, poetry, painting, and music.

You may contact Ben W. Johnson by using the information listed below.

CONTACT INFO

My Eduka Solutions
330 W. Main St. # 214
Middletown, PA, Zip: 17057

EMAIL INFO

E-mail Address: benjohnson@gmail.com

SOCIAL MEDIA INFO

Find Dr. Ben Wood Johnson on the following media platforms.

Twitter handle: @benwoodpost
Facebook Page: @benwoodpost

PERSONAL WEBSITES

Official blog site: www.benwoodpost.com
Official website: www.benwoodjohnson.com
Official Book Store: www.benwoodjbooks.com

INDEX

Below are some of the words and phrases that had been echoed throughout the text.

PUBLISHED WORKS

Published works by Dr. Ben Wood Johnson include the following:

1. Racism: What is it?

2. Sartrean Ethics: A Defense of Jean-Paul Sartre as a Moral Philosopher

3. Jean-Paul Sartre and Morality: A Legacy Under Attack

4. Sartre Lives On

5. Forced Out of Vietnam: A Policy Analysis of the Fall of Saigon

6. Natural Law : Morality and Obedience

7. Cogito Ergo Philosophus

8. Citizen Obedience: The Nature of Legal Obligation

9. Le Racisme et le Socialisme : La Discrimination Raciale dans un Milieu Capitaliste

10. International Law : The Rise of Russia as a Global Threat

11. Être Noir: Quel Malheur!

12. L'homme et le Racisme : Être Responsable de vos Actions et Omissions

OTHER PUBLICATIONS

1. Studying While Black in America: The Chronicles of an Adult Learner

2. François Gaya: The Chronicles of an Immigrant

3. Preserving Your Beingness: The Chronicles of a Survivalist

4. Madame De Rouleau

Published by TESKO PUBLISHING
A subsidiary of MY EDUKA SOLUTIONS

www.benwoodpost.com

www.ingramcontent.com/pod-product-compliance
Lightning Source LLC
Chambersburg PA
CBHW022119280326
41933CB00007B/459